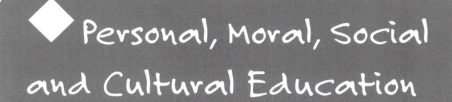
◆ Personal, Moral, Social and Cultural Education

GROWING UP TODAY

Me as a person

Key Stage 2/P4-7

Carole Barnickle and Duncan Wilson

HOPSCOTCH
H
EDUCATIONAL PUBLISHING

◆ Contents

Published by Hopscotch Educational Publishing Company Ltd, 29 Waterloo Place, Leamington Spa CV32 5LA 01926 744227

© 2000 Hopscotch Educational Publishing

Written by Carole Barnickle and Duncan Wilson
Design by Steve Williams
Illustrated by Cathy Gilligan
Cover illustration by Cathy Gilligan
Printed by Clintplan, Southam

Carole Barnickle and Duncan Wilson hereby assert their moral right to be identified as the authors of this work in accordance with the Copyright, Designs and Patents Act, 1988.

ISBN 1-902239-39-3

◆ Introduction

This book is one of a set of four books, each looking at a different area of the DfEE's recommendations for the teaching of PSHE and Citizenship at Key Stage Two. In these books we are trying to share ideas with colleagues. We hope you will find something that you are able to use in your school.

We work at a three-form entry Junior School in Bourrville, Birmingham. We have been actively involved in promoting citizenship throughout our school for the past four years.

Many of you may be wondering:
◆ what citizenship is
◆ how you can fit citizenship into an already overcrowded timetable
◆ what activities you can use to promote citizenship in your school

We think that citizenship in schools is about giving children the skills to become responsible individuals and independent thinkers. They should be able to make informed judgments that will enhance their quality of life and that of others, while, at all times, showing respect for themselves and other people, irrespective of gender, culture, religion and ethnicity.

While we realise that this is quite a challenge we feel that these are important skills that have long been neglected and can be taught across the curriculum. Although these lessons stand alone, we feel that they also lend themselves to the Literacy Hour or as part of an RE scheme of work.

In our school, circle time is well established as part of the weekly timetable. For colleagues not familiar with circle time, the concept was first developed by Jenny Mosley (see 'Quality Circle Time' published by Learning Development Aids). Jenny developed the concept to help schools effect individual and organisational change. The aim is to empower everyone in the school community to have an equal voice in the discussion, recognition or game being used through the use of various strategies.

In our school it is a time of the week when the classroom becomes much less formal, allowing the teacher and children the opportunity to get to know one another, develop team building skills, play co-operation games and present and discuss views.

We have a very active School Council made up of representatives from each class. We are also involved with the local Development Education Centre. Our school Debating Society discusses issues raised by the children and many of our children have had the opportunity to attend debates at the Council House. Our assemblies reflect citizenship issues.

For a school to be successful in its delivery of the citizenship curriculum it has to have a whole-school approach to the subject. We feel very strongly that it is not a subject that can be taught once a week, but that it should be reflected in the whole ethos of the school and in the attitudes expressed by the pupils and staff. We feel that the development of these attitudes among the children is the key to monitoring the success of your citizenship programme.

Where do you begin?
Circle time

Our school began by introducing circle time into the timetable, using this as a means for the children to raise and discuss their worries and concerns surrounding such issues as bullying, friendship groups and name calling, in a non-threatening environment. We found that it was also a useful tool for helping Year 3 children get over the transfer from Infant to Junior School.

Rules are established at the beginning of the session. Generally there are three rules, the first being that a person only speaks when they are holding the magic object (we have a dinosaur egg teddy which turns inside out into a baby dinosaur), the second being that everyone else must listen when another person is talking and the third being that if someone does not want to speak they are not pressured to and can 'pass' their turn on to the next. It is up to you whether or not you add further rules to specific discussions. For example, if discussing the issue of bullying it might be reasonable to set the rule that no-one can use any names.

You will see that in many of the chapters we have recommended that the children are to be seated as for circle time. Given the constraints of many classrooms, it is up to you to decide how it would work best for you. Circle time sessions can be run with the class and teacher seated in a circle on the floor, with the class at their desks or with the children facing you sitting down.

The School Council

Our School Council was started in order to give the children a voice, allowing them to raise any concerns they had about their time in school with the two teacher representatives who also sit on the Council. It has proved to be a very effective way for children to communicate with teachers and vice versa. We have undertaken projects in school and the community that have been suggested, organised and run by the Council representatives. The Council meets once a fortnight for half an hour during lunch and the children have gradually taken on the roles of chairperson and secretary. Council representatives are elected by the class and are changed each year.

We have noticed that children sitting on the Council have become more confident and articulate because they have been elected by their classmates to present the views of their class to the Council. If children in our classes have concerns, we encourage them to put these concerns to their representative, who will then raise and discuss them at the next meeting.

Circle time and a School Council are two ways that you can start to challenge the attitudes of the children and staff in your school. We also hope that using the ideas in this book will make a difference.

Using this book

The chapters are all set out in the same way. Each begins with a focus for the chapter which contains the learning objectives taken from the 'National Curriculum Framework for PSHE and Citizenship'.

These are followed by key points and notes for teachers detailing our thoughts about the concepts being taught. We have tried to anticipate and discuss some of the problems colleagues might have and, as practising teachers, we have suggested strategies that we have used to help us deliver the material with sensitivity.

After this are two lesson plans, one each for younger and older children. By younger children we mean Years 3 and 4 and by older children we mean Years 5 and 6. Each lesson plan follows the format of a whole-class introductiory session, suggestions for group work followed by a plenary session and includes two differentiated photocopiable worksheets.

Several chapters also give details of generic sheets and these are to be found at the back of the book. At the end of each chapter are suggestions for further activities that could be undertaken relating to the chapter focus.

We have not suggested a time schedule for the lessons, but you could adopt a three-part format of introduction, development and plenary. We recommend that each lesson should last approximately one hour. Many of the lessons lend themselves to more than one session and could be developed over several weeks.

About each chapter

Chapter 1: Thinking about me

◆ Younger children will become more aware of themselves as individuals by considering their characteristics, but will learn to listen to and appreciate the experiences of others. They will begin to appreciate the link between achieving a task and being happy.

◆ Older children will begin to recognise and value their achievements. They will begin to self evaluate and set themselves targets for the future. They will have a clearer understanding that everyone achieves at their own level and in different areas of their lives. They will recognise that they have different strengths, but that they are all equally valuable.

Chapter 2: A future me

◆ Younger children will develop their understanding of the range of jobs in society, they will start to recognise that certain jobs require specific skills and they will begin to consider a job they would like to do and the skills they would need to develop to be able to do that job effectively.

◆ Older children will recognise that certain jobs require specific skills and that many jobs require different skills.

Chapter 3: A confident me

◆ Younger children will learn how to express an opinion, they will develop their ability to listen sensibly and respectfully to other people expressing their opinions and they will learn about a topic in the wider community.

◆ Older children will learn how to express an opinion about a range of issues, they will begin to recognise the importance of having an opinion and they will develop their ability to listen sensibly and respectfully to other people expressing their opinions.

Chapter 4: Making decisions for me

◆ Younger children will recognise that decisions cannot always be made by themselves and that the decisions they do make will have consequences for themselves and for other people.

◆ Older children will begin to realise that they have a choice, that they can say no and the consequences of not making the right decision. They will begin to appreciate the importance of making an informed decision.

Chapter 5: Understanding a changing me

◆ Younger children will develop their understanding about a range of emotions and will begin to recognise that as they get older the range of emotions they feel and the situations in which they feel them, become more complex.

◆ Older children will consider and reflect on the emotions they experience and will begin to recognise when other people experience the same emotions. The children will be encouraged to reflect on situations and to acknowledge that their actions affect the emotional experiences of others.

Chapter 6: A money-minded me

◆ Younger children will learn about the importance of not spending all their money in one go. They will learn that they have choices and that they have to live by the consequences of the choices they make.

◆ Older children will reflect on the money they spend and on the importance of saving. They will begin to recognise that adults need money to provide for their everyday needs.

◆Thinking about me

Focus

◆ 1b. To develop self esteem, confidence, independence and responsibility and make the most of their abilities, pupils should be taught to recognise their worth as individuals by expressing positive things about themselves and their achievements, seeing their mistakes and setting personal goals.

Key issue: Why do we need to think about ourselves?

◆ Everybody is better at doing some things than others. The aim of this chapter is to help children to think about what abilities they have and to recognise their strengths.

◆ They should be encouraged to think about and respect the strengths and weaknesses of their friends and classmates.

◆ When weaknesses have been identified they should be encouraged to discuss how these might be addressed.

◆ They should be encouraged to explore their own feelings about other people to investigate how those people might feel about them.

Notes for teachers

Children are very poor at recognising their strengths and yet each of them would be able to discuss with their parents or teachers what they and their friends are not very good at. The purpose of this chapter is to encourage children to reflect on themselves, to recognise their strengths and to come to terms with their weaknesses. The activities will encourage them to express themselves as individuals while still respecting the right of others to express themselves. They will develop an understanding of their role within the larger group, be it in the classroom, the school, or their community.

Of all the people in the world, some wear glasses and some don't, some wear the right clothes and accessories and others don't, some people are sporty or intelligent or artistic and creative and other people aren't. These attributes are commonly seen as being favourable or unfavourable when linked with people. As we grow up we often use these attributes to judge a person. Early on, children recognise that there are others who have different attributes from them and they begin to categorise their peers according to those who are similar and those who are essentially different.

Some children have the strength of character and self-assurance to disregard such unfavourable attention. Others take it to heart. As teachers, it is essential that we help these children to recognise their worth as individuals and to understand that they are valued for themselves and their personalities rather than just for certain favourable characteristics.

◇ ◆ ◇ ◆ ◇ ◆ ◇ ◆ Thinking about me ◆ ◇ ◆ ◇ ◆ ◇ ◆ ◇ ◆ ◇ ◆ ◇ ◆ ◇ ◆ ◇

Intended outcomes

◆ The children will become more aware of themselves as individuals by considering their characteristics, but will learn to listen to and appreciate the experiences of others. They will begin to appreciate the link between achieving a task and being happy.

Resources

◆ shoe box
◆ mirror
◆ pencils
◆ the photocopiable activity sheets on pages 8 and 9
◆ crayons
◆ a picture of a celebrity

Lesson plan for younger children

Introduction

◆ Sit the children in a circle preferably on the floor. Tell them that you are very proud of them because they have... (done something very special). Encourage them to tell the class the things that they value about their friends. Build up a picture of what makes a valued friend. Discuss strengths and weaknesses. Can they identify any of these characteristics in themselves?

Questions to ask:
◆ Think of a good friend. Why do you like them?
◆ Why do you think people like you?
◆ Do you think there are things about you that people don't like?
◆ Have you achieved something that you had to work really hard for?
◆ How do you feel when you get things right/wrong?

◆ Introduce a famous person using a picture, for example a popular footballer. Who would like to be similar to this person and why? What makes the person so special? What characteristics does he/she have that make so many people admire him/her? Say that you would like to introduce them to someone who is equally special, who also has valued characteristics and skills that will in the future help them to achieve many things. Pass around the shoe box. Make the children promise that they will not show anyone else what is inside the box. As they look in, they will see a mirror reflecting their own face.

Group activities

Photocopiable activity sheet 1

This sheet is more suitable for lower ability children. They should think about themselves and what they are like, for example patient or quick-tempered. They should then draw a picture of themselves in the first box and write about themselves. In the second box they should draw what they can do (their achievements) and write about them. In the last section they should draw and write about what they want to achieve.

Photocopiable activity sheet 2

Using this sheet, more able children draw two pictures, one of themselves and one of an imaginary friend and write the characteristics and hobbies they have and those that they would like their imaginary friend to have. They then compare the two sets of characteristics identifying those that are the same and those that are different.

Plenary session

Write up some of the characteristics that the children feel they have, then the characteristics that they would like to have. Discuss what they would have to do to develop the skills to achieve their goals.

Questions to ask:
◆ What are you like?
◆ What would you like to be?
◆ What will you have to do to achieve this?
◆ How do people get better at things? Talk about not giving up and working hard.

◆ About me ◆

About me

Me

_____

_____

_____

_____

_____

I can

_____

_____

_____

_____

_____

I can do this

I would like to

_____

_____

_____

_____

I want to do this

PHOTOCOPIABLE PAGE

◆ Me and my friend ◆

◆ Think about a friend you would like to have. Draw pictures of both of you. Around the pictures describe your characteristics and hobbies.

I like to

_____

_____

I like to

_____

_____

My eyes are

_____

_____

My hair is

_____

My first language is

_____

_____

My friend's hair is

_____

My friend likes to

_____

_____

My friend's eyes are

_____

_____

My friend's first language is

_____

_____

My friend likes to

_____

_____

◆ Now write about what you can both do and what your friend can do that you would like to do.

We both

_____

_____

My friend can _____ I wish I could.

My friend can _____ I wish I could.

◆ On the back of this sheet write you think you need to do to be like your friend.

◆Thinking about me

Intended outcomes

◆ The children will begin to recognise and value their achievements. They will begin to self evaluate and set themselves targets for the future. They will have a clearer understanding that everyone achieves at their own level and in different areas of their lives. They will recognise that they have different strengths, but that they are all equally valuable.

Resources

◆ pencils and crayons
◆ the photocopiable activity sheets on pages 11 and 12

Lesson plan for older children

Introduction

◆ Sit the children in a circle so that they have eye contact with each other, preferably on the floor. Start off by telling the children something that they have achieved and should be proud of. Each child should tell the person sitting next to them one thing that they are proud of having achieved. Then each child takes it in turns to tell the rest of the class their neighbour's achievement. Ask them what thing they would like to be able to do in the future. Discuss what they think they will have to do to accomplish their goal.

Questions to ask:
◆ What is an achievement?
◆ How did you feel when you achieved your goal?
◆ How do you feel about achieving your future goal?
◆ What will you have to do in order to achieve your future goal?
◆ What stops you from doing the things you want to do?

◆ Explain that different people have different goals in life and have achieved different things. For example, we are not all going to score or want to score goals for our country, and we may not feel the same sense of achievement as someone who does. In the same way, they are not going to feel the same sense of achievement as we do when we swim five metres, if that has been our goal. The excitement and satisfaction felt are relative to the individual person.

Group activities
Photocopiable activity sheet 1
Lower ability children will record things they feel they have achieved. They then think about the things that they would like to be able to do in the future.

Photocopiable activity sheet 2
More able children complete a pathway that takes them through their lives detailing their achievements from birth to present day. They should give reasons for their choices. For example, how did they make them/their family/their friends feel? Did they succeed in doing something they had previously not been able to do/ found challenging?

Plenary session
◆ How do we feel when we achieve something new?
◆ Do we all want the same things?
◆ How do we feel when we/one of our friends achieves a goal?
◆ Why aren't we all good at the same things/everything?
◆ Does it matter if we want to achieve different things to our friends?
◆ Have we all achieved something or is it something only certain people do?

◆ About me ◆

◆ Complete the sentences and draw pictures to show your achievements.

At home   **At school**

The best thing I ever did…
At home
_____
_____
At school
_____
_____

Last week I did this…
At home
_____
_____
At school
_____
_____

Yesterday I did this…
At home
_____
_____
At school
_____
_____

What I want to do…
At home
_____
_____
At school
_____
_____

◆ My road through life ◆

◆ Complete the journey from birth to today in words and pictures. Show what you have achieved as you have grown older. Write your age at each stage.

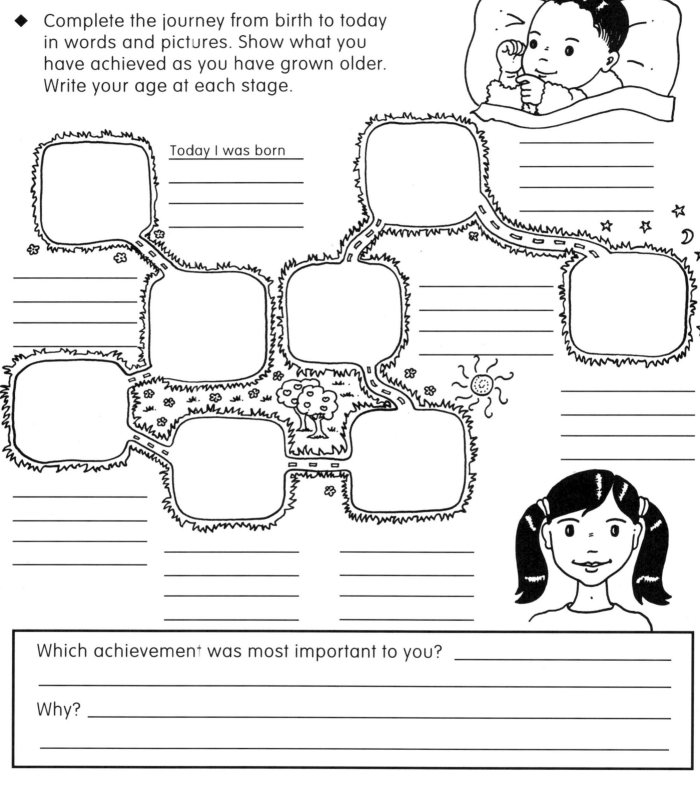

Today I was born

Which achievement was most important to you? _____

_____

Why? _____

_____

◆ On the back of this sheet, draw and write about what you would like to achieve in the future. Think about learning to drive, getting a job or going to university or college.

Further activities to develop understanding

◆ Encourage the children to draw up lists of characteristics they consider to be personal strengths. Ask them to select their top six. Ask them to think of things they do not consider to be strengths and select three of these as areas they would like to improve on. They should share the two lists with a friend to see if he/she agrees with what has been written.

◆ In pairs, the children could build up a word box of vocabulary for describing people and emotions. Ask them to write a circle of feelings around an appropriately smiling or scowling face. Write the situation in the centre of the face. Situations might include how the child feels when they are picked on/called names/with their friends/at home and so on.

◆ Ask the children to consider confidence by completing the following statements: I feel confident when... I don't feel confident when... They should then answer these questions: What could my family/friends/teacher do to make me feel more confident? What do people do that makes me lose confidence? Use the generic sheet on page 54.

◆ Ask the children to consider the nature of happiness. I feel happy when... I feel unhappy when... What could I do to make myself happier? What could my family/friends/teacher do to make me feel happier? How do I see myself? How do others see me? I feel valued when... I don't feel valued when...

◆ Discuss people the children admire. What is it about these people that makes the children respect them? Is it the way they behave, dress or what they do? Collect pictures of people from magazines and sort them. Discuss the nature of the person. Do we really know these people? Discuss whether they are correct to make these assumptions about other people.

◆ Encourage the children to write personal lists. What do I know about myself? How would I describe myself to other people? How would other people describe me? Do other people describe me in these terms because of the way I behave/treat other people myself? Are there things that we don't know about ourselves? Do we have habits we are unaware of?

◆A future me

Focus

◆ Developing confidence and responsibility and making the most of their abilities, pupils should be taught: 1e) about the range of jobs carried out by people they know, and to understand how they can develop skills to make their own contribution in the future.

Key issue: Why do we need to think about our future?

◆ Children should be encouraged to work towards targets.
◆ Children should learn about a wide range of jobs and opportunities within their community.

Notes for teachers

Parents and carers have a responsibility to ensure that the children in their care develop the skills, knowledge and understanding to become independent young people, capable of taking an active part in today's society. This process starts with newborn babies when they are helped to reach specific milestones in their development. For example, a confident crawler is helped to stand in preparation for the first steps. A young child is helped to gain the confidence required to ride a bicycle by the addition of stabilisers or by the hand of an adult on the saddle. These props are then removed when the child is ready. This continues throughout childhood with children meeting their targets, helped along by a caring adult.

As they grow older, children should be allowed to take responsibility for aspects of their lives and make decisions about the skills they would like to and need to develop. They should be helped to realise the importance of working hard to achieve goals as preparation for the role they are to take in society as an adult.

Professionally, we are called upon to set academic targets for the children in our care. Teachers should be aware that they are becoming increasingly accountable for the achievements of children in their classes. Targets are made to be met!

In the short term we ask our children to set themselves goals that will help them to improve in a chosen field. By this we mean academic subjects, sports, creative arts, interpersonal and social skills. In the long term, we want them to attain the best quality of life while maintaining a balance between their own happiness and needs and those of the wider community and environment.

A part of this process is teaching the children about the roles people play in society. A starting point for young children can be the structure of the school, across the whole range of jobs available (secretary, cooks, cleaners, caretaker as well as teachers). From this point the children should look at the jobs held by people in their local community and family.

We can extend this to jobs in the wider community and at national and global levels. More able children can be helped to categorise these jobs into those in the service, industrial, entertainment and commercial sectors.

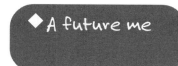

Intended outcomes

◆ The children will develop their understanding of the range of jobs in society and will start to recognise that certain jobs require certain skills. They will begin to consider a job they would like to do and the skills they would need to develop to be able to do that job effectively.

Resources

◆ the photocopiable activity sheets on pages 16 and 17

Lesson plan for younger children

Introduction

◆ Ask the children what they would like to do when they are older. Record some of their ideas on the board. You could use different coloured chalks/pens to distinguish between jobs in the service, manufacturing, commercial and entertainment sectors. This can be returned to during the plenary session.

◆ Discuss people the children know who hold these jobs and what they think the jobs involve.

Group activities

Tell the children that you are going to give them an activity sheet to complete. Explain that in the first section they are asked to write the job they would like to do when they leave school. Tell them that when this has been completed, they will be asked to consider the skills that would be needed to do/perform other jobs.

Photocopiable activity sheet 1

This sheet is for less able children. After writing what job they want to do when they leave school, they are asked to connect a series of small pictures representing people at work with the skills required to do the job effectively. They are then asked to draw a small picture of themselves doing the job they would like to do and then write the skills they think they will need to develop to do it.

Photocopiable activity sheet 2

The more able children are to consider and discuss with a partner the skills that they already have and those that they think they will need to target as they grow older. They should record these on the sheet.

Plenary session

When the children have completed their sheets, ask some of them to present to the class what their partner would like to do, the skills they think they have and the skills they think they will need to target. To close the lesson, agree with the children that certain jobs require certain skills (use the jobs and skills already collated on the board) and that if they are really interested in getting their ideal job, they will need to develop the relevant skills as they grow older. Can they think of humorous examples of unsuitable candidates for a range of jobs? For example, someone who doesn't like children becoming a teacher!

◆ Skills for a job ◆

◆ Write here the job you want to do when you are older.

_____

◆ Different jobs require different skills. What skills are needed to do the jobs pictured below? Draw a line from each job to its skills.

◆ Be able to talk to people.
◆ Be able to follow instructions.
◆ Be able to work out money problems.

◆ Like doing practical tasks.
◆ Be able to work on your own.
◆ Be able to work things out.

◆ Like working with people.
◆ Not mind the sight of blood.
◆ Be kind and caring.

◆ Write about the skills you will need to do the job you want to do.

_____

_____

_____

_____

This is a picture of me as a

_____

PHOTOCOPIABLE PAGE

◆ Skills for a job ◆

◆ Write here the job you want to do when you are older.

_____

◆ Different jobs require different skills. What skills do you have?
Talk to a friend about what they think your skills are.

My best skills

● _____

● _____

● _____

◆ Now think about the job you would like to have. What skills are
needed to do this job?

● _____

● _____

● _____

◆ What skills do you need to learn? Set yourself three targets.

● _____

● _____

● _____

A future me

Intended outcomes

◆ The children will recognise that certain jobs require specific skills and that many jobs require different skills.

Resources

◆ the photocopiable activity sheets on pages 19 and 20

Lesson plan for older children

Introduction

◆ Ask the children to think about and discuss the skills required to teach. These ideas can be written on the board.

◆ Then lead a discussion about the skills required in another job, for example a professional athlete, an office- or shop-worker or a nurse. Discuss the differences between the jobs and the skills that are required to do both. Encourage the children to use the following words: respect, responsibility, honesty, patience, caring, service, professionalism.

Group activities
Photocopiable activity sheet 1

This sheet is for less able children. They are asked to match descriptions to jobs and try to name the job described. They should write the name underneath the description and draw a picture showing someone carrying out the job. Underneath the picture they also write down what the person is doing.

Photocopiable activity sheet 2

This sheet is for more able children who should match skills to specific jobs. Choosing from the list of skills in the box, they should find three skills relevant to each of the jobs pictured. They write each skill in the box next to the picture. They should then discuss each job and decide upon two additional skills that they feel each would require. As an extension activity the children are asked to list five skills they feel they have and then write down the jobs they feel their skills would match.

Plenary session

Collate the skills identified by the class. Ask one child to select a particular skill that he or she would like to develop and, as a class, share strategies about how to develop it. Repeat this with another child.

◆ Which job? ◆

◆ Read the job descriptions and decide who would do each one. Then draw a picture of someone doing the job and complete the sentences.

I am a very caring person. I like to look after people. I do not mind clearing up after accidents and I can stay calm when people are upset or hurt.

This is a picture of a _____ who is _____

_____

I like animals. I help to make them better. I am kind to animals and people. I understand how people feel when they are worried. I have a lot of patience. I am good at science.

This is a picture of a _____ who is _____

_____

I am very honest. I am fit and responsible. I like helping people to be safe. I know all about the law.

This is a picture of a _____ who is _____

_____

◆ On the back of this sheet, draw a picture of a job you would like to do. Write a list of skills needed to do the job.

◆ Skills for the job ◆

◆ Look at the pictures of people doing their jobs. Select three skills for each job from the list in the box. Write them next to the pictures. Think of two other skills for each job and write them as well.

responsible; caring; confident; honest; fit; patient; team player; prefers to work alone; works hard; can manage people; can organise paperwork; can organise people; good at maths/English/ science; good at exams; practical; can share; likes to work indoors/ outdoors.

● _____

● _____

● _____

● _____

● _____

● _____

● _____

● _____

● _____

● _____

● _____

● _____

● _____

● _____

● _____

● _____

● _____

● _____

● _____

● _____

◆ On the back of this sheet, list five skills that you have and write down the jobs they would match.

PHOTOCOPIABLE PAGE   Hopscotch ◆ Me as a person

Further activities to develop understanding

◆ Brainstorm all the jobs that the children are aware of and classify jobs identified into related groups such as service, commercial, entertainment and manufacturing. Working in groups, the children could choose one of the jobs then design an advertisement which lists the skills required. See the generic sheet on page 55.

◆ Discuss and identify the social, physical, practical, language, scientific, research and creative skills that the children have. Identify and discuss pupils' strengths, weaknesses and interests.

◆ Discuss whether certain jobs are more/less suitable for different groups of people. The teacher should encourage children to come to the conclusion that everybody should have the same opportunities in the job market.

◆ Invite visitors into the school to discuss jobs held. Build up a portfolio of jobs and skills that the children are aware of.

◆ Many authorities actively encourage the development of links between schools and businesses. Often these organisations will allow children to tour their premises.

◆ Brainstorm all the jobs in the school. Small groups of children can then be asked to focus on one of the jobs identified and write down the most important skills that they feel the person holding the job needs. These skills should then be recorded on the board.

◆ Discuss with the children the sorts of jobs they would be interested in. Talk about the qualifications that would be needed for some of these. Say that when they want to apply for a job, they usually have to fill in an application form. Give them copies of the generic sheet on page 56. Explain the terminology they may not understand, such as 'Relevant qualifications'. Help them to complete their forms.

◆A confident me

Focus

◆ Developing confidence and responsibility, and making the most of their abilities, pupils should be taught 1a) to talk and write about their opinions, and explain their views on issues that affect themselves and society.

Key issue: Why do we need to be able to express our own opinions and respect those of others?

◆ Children should be encouraged to express their opinions with confidence. They should be taught to listen to and respect the opinions of others.

Notes for teachers

At an early age, children learn how to express their needs. For example when they are hungry or thirsty they will let someone know. As they grow older they should be encouraged to think about the wider needs of society and start to formulate opinions on different subjects that are relevant to their lives and the world they live in. They should be encouraged to consider issues such as:

◆ Should more children be walking to school?
◆ Should children go to school on Saturday mornings?
◆ Should people be fined for dropping litter?

While encouraging children to develop rational, wide ranging opinions, we feel that they must learn to state these opinions with sensitivity and respect for other people and their opinions and feelings. Children should recognise that they should speak differently to adults from the way they speak to their peers.

We must also teach them to consider broader issues when expressing opinions. For example, a child might want to be allowed to stay up late watching television, but from the point of view of their health and wellbeing, they should be encouraged to get a good night's sleep.

We are all aware of children who are reluctant to speak in front of others. We feel that it is important that they should be encouraged, but not forced into contributing. Circle time offers a less threatening situation in which we can encourage children to air their opinions.

We should allow children to develop their own opinions. At the same time we must help them to recognise that there are rules and conventions held by society that are there to ensure their health, safety and personal development. These rules are for their protection and should be respected. For example, 12-year-old children might want to watch an 18 certificate film, not realising that the restriction is in place to protect them from unsuitable content that would be disturbing for some children.

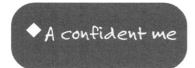

◆ A confident me

Intended outcomes

◆ The children will express an opinion about a possession, they will listen to other people expressing their opinions sensibly and respectfully and they will begin to form an opinion about a topic in the wider community.

Resources

◆ a favourite possession for each child in the class and the teacher
◆ newspaper cuttings showing letters from readers expressing opinions
◆ the photocopiable worksheets on pages 24 and 25

Lesson plan for younger children

Introduction

◆ Seat the class as for a circle time activity. Ask the children to introduce their toy to the rest of the class. Encourage them to describe it to the class. When the first round has been completed, ask the children to tell the class why they have brought this particular toy into school and what it is about the toy that makes it their favourite. Help them to set the appropriate tone by discussing your own toy/possession at the start of each round.

◆ When the round has been completed, tell the class that they have been expressing an opinion about their favourite toy. An opinion is when we make a decision based on personal choice and judgment. Tell them that they will be doing further work on looking at their opinions during the rest of the lesson.

Group activities
The photocopiable activity sheets

Introduce the worksheets to the class. They both contain the same challenges but **Activity sheet 1** contains a lower language level and asks for fewer examples from the children. **Activity sheet 2** is more advanced, requiring more writing. Both sheets contain the statement: 'All children should be made to walk to and from school.' The children should work together in pairs or small groups to discuss this, then record their ideas on the sheet. These ideas should be recorded whether they are for or against the statement as they represent the opinion held by the individuals in the group. Help the groups as required. After five to ten minutes' discussion, bring the class back together and collect ideas on the board, discussing and clarifying as required.

Plenary session

Begin the plenary session by explaining to the class that we hold opinions about everything from our favourite toy/football team/sweets to the games we should play or the people we should play with. Read some letters from a newspaper from people writing in and expressing their opinions. End the lesson by telling the class that it is not the person who can shout the loudest who is heard, but the person who can express their opinions most intelligently and interestingly.

◆ Agree or disagree? ◆

◆ Read this statement.

> All children should be made to walk to and from school.

◆ Many people think that children should be made to walk to and from school. Do you agree or disagree? Put a ✔.

Agree [ ]   Disagree [ ]

◆ Write three reasons why you think this.

I think this because _____

_____

I think this because _____

_____

I think this because _____

_____

◆ Now think of a reason why someone might not agree with you.

I think people might not agree with me because they think that _____

_____

◆ Would you like to have to walk to and from school every day? Say why.

_____

_____

_____

PHOTOCOPIABLE PAGE   Hopscotch ◆ Me as a person

◆ Agree or disagree? ◆

◆ Read this statement.

> All children should be made to walk to and from school.

◆ Think carefully about the statement. Do you think it is fair or unfair?

◆ Give three reasons to support the statement.

- ● _____

- ● _____

- ● _____

◆ Give three reasons against the statement.

- ● _____

- ● _____

- ● _____

◆ What do you think? Prepare a short paragraph to either support or disagree with the statement. You may be asked to share your views with the class. Remember to give reasons why you agree or disagree.

I think

◇ ◆ ◇ ◆ ◇ ◆ ◇ ◆ ◇ ◆ ◇ ◆ ◇ ◆ ◇ ◆ ◇ ◆ ◇ ◆ ◇ ◆ ◇ ◆ ◇ ◆ ◇

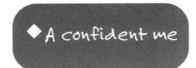
A confident me

Intended outcomes

◆ The children will express an opinion about a range of issues, they will begin to recognise the importance of having an opinion and they will listen to other people expressing their opinions sensibly and respectfully.

Resources

◆ the photocopiable activity sheets on pages 27 and 28

Lesson plan for older children

This lesson could be used as a starting point for projects investigating other countries that are democracies and for countries that are not democracies. The children could also investigate people who fight to defend their opinions and their rights.

Introduction

◆ As a class, discuss what an opinion is and try to put together a definition everyone agrees with.

◆ Tell the children that one of the ways organisations find out about what people think is by asking them to complete questionnaires. Ask them why they think that organisations need this information and what the purpose is behind the questionnaires. Explain that opinions are sought on a whole range of issues from the nature of a product and how that product is packaged, to government policies and legislation.

Group activities

Tell the children that they are going to complete a questionnaire. On these they will express their opinions about a range of issues from those involving the school to those involving the wider community. They will then try to explain why they think as they do and justify the opinions they have expressed.

Photocopiable activity sheet 1

This sheet is for less able children. They are required to work in pairs to read several statements and indicate those with which they agree and disagree. They are then asked to produce a short piece of writing about one of the statements.

Photocopiable activity sheet 2

This sheet is for more able children. They are asked to write in greater detail their responses to the same statements as on Activity sheet 1.

Plenary session

Collate the children's responses to the statements on the sheets and write the results on the board. Ask some children to explain why they think the way they do. Hold a short discussion with the class on whether or not they agree. Discuss the concept of having a class opinion. Explain that we live in a democracy. In a democratic society people have the right to vote for their representatives. The politician or councillor who gets the most votes is elected to the government or council. The decision is made according to what the majority of the people want.

◆ For or against? ◆

Do you think
'Yes'?
(for)

Do you think
'No'?
(against)

◆ Read these sentences with a friend. Talk about them together. If you agree with the statements, underline them in red. If you disagree, underline them in blue.

- All children should be made to walk to and from school.

- Boys should do one hour of homework each night. Girls should do two hours of homework every night.

- Children under eight years old should be sent to bed before 7 o'clock each evening.

- The school day should begin at 8.00am and end at 5.00pm.

- All children should make their own beds and keep their rooms clean and tidy.

- All children should be given £5 pocket money every week no matter what their age.

◆ Now choose one of the statements you have underlined in blue and give three reasons why you disagree with it.

- _____

- _____

- _____

◆ For or against? ◆

Do you think
'Yes'?
(for)

Do you think
'No'?
(against)

◆ Look at each of these statements. Decide if you are 'for' or 'against' them. Give reasons for your decisions.

● All children should be made to walk to and from school. | for/against |

I think this because _____

_____

● Boys should do one hour of homework each night. Girls should | for/against | do two hours of homework every night.

I think this because _____

_____

● Children under eight years old should be sent to bed before | for/against | 7 o'clock each evening.

I think this because _____

_____

● The school day should begin at 8.00am and end at 5.00pm. | for/against |

I think this because _____

_____

● All children should make their own beds and keep their | for/against | rooms clean and tidy.

I think this because _____

_____

● All children should be given £5 pocket money every week | for/against | no matter what their age.

I think this because _____

_____

Further activities to develop understanding

◆ What issues do the children consider to be important? Are they personal or social? Are they local, domestic or global? What can the children do to find out about these issues? What might happen if they don't find out about these issues? How can other people help them to find out about the issues?

◆ Help the children to realise that if they have concerns about specific issues there are people and organisations who can help, such as teachers, parents, relatives, the RSPCA and so on. Show them examples of people's letters to the press expressing concerns.

◆ Hold a class debate on who the children respect and why and who they do not respect and why.

◆ Ask the children to consider how we should listen and talk to other people and why? Should we talk to different people in different ways? Why?

◆ Organise and run a debate in the classroom using the ideas from the generic sheet on page 57. Let the children choose the debate or pick one out of a hat.

◆ Give the children copies of the generic sheet on page 58. On the top half of the sheet they draw pictures and complete positive statements about themselves. At the bottom of the sheet they write sentences and draw pictures of their targets for improvement.

◆ Repeat the above activity, but encourage the children to add a phrase beginning: 'because...' to the end of each sentence. Ask them to write at the bottom of the sheet things that they and other people could do to help them get over their lack of confidence with these activities.

◆ Ask the children to complete a letter to a newspaper agony aunt giving an example of when they found themselves in a situation in which they lacked confidence. They or a friend should then write a reply letter from the agony aunt giving advice as to how they could have helped themselves in this situation.

◆Making decisions for me

Focus

◆ Developing confidence and responsibility, and making the most of their abilities, pupils should be taught 1c) to face new challenges positively through collecting information, looking for help, making responsible choices, and taking action.

Key issue: How can we make informed decisions?

Notes for teachers

We all need to make decisions every day of our lives. As adults we make decisions guided by previous knowledge of similar situations. We learn how to handle situations in a more sensitive manner after we have previously experienced conflict in those situations. The decisions we make are affected by our previous experiences.

As teachers we are often faced with potentially professionally-challenging scenarios with children, parents, carers and colleagues. Experience helps us to learn how to handle these incidents more productively should they happen again in the future. Experiences and discussions with friends, colleagues and relatives teach us strategies for calming situations from the start, for regaining control, for what to say and what not to say and also an awareness of how to keep ourselves safe in the event that the situation escalates.

Some decisions need to be more carefully considered and even researched, because they fall outside our experience. Adults are able to set themselves goals and targets to work towards and make the appropriate decisions to reach those goals.

We must begin to give our children, at a very early age, the skills and confidence to make the appropriate decisions for themselves. We must challenge them to set their own goals and to develop the strategies and the stamina to achieve these.

At a young age, children are able to say that they would like to get better at a specific thing and are able to say how they think they would get better at this. For example, children who want to learn how to ride a bicycle or play the recorder realise that the only way they will get better is by practising. They make the decision to carry on rather than give up.

We can extend this into the classroom by encouraging our children to set themselves academic targets, such as improving their reading or handwriting. If we involve them in this decision-making process, they are more likely to achieve their aims. The children have a sense of ownership and this makes the decision they have made more meaningful.

As children get older the decisions they make become more personal and they begin to make personal lifestyle choices, such as their religion, whether or not to become a vegetarian and what political party to support. We must give them the skills, knowledge and understanding to make informed decisions on these matters.

◆Making decisions for me

Intended outcomes

◆ The children will recognise that decisions cannot always be made by themselves and that the decisions that they do make will have consequences for themselves and for other people.

Resources

◆ the photocopiable activity sheets on pages 32 and 33
◆ the story on pages 59 and 60

Lesson plan for younger children

Introduction

◆ Read the class the story on pages 59 and 60 and ask them to listen very carefully for any decisions that have to be made by or for the characters in the story. When the story has been finished, discuss and collect on the board the decisions the children have identified. Who has made the decisions? The class should then discuss the consequences of the decisions that were made in the story. Do they think any of the characters in the story made the wrong decision? Why? (The story could be photocopied and given to pairs of children so that they can underline the decisions made.)

Group activities

Organise the children into ability groups and give them the photocopiable activity sheets. These ask them to consider the consequences of the decisions they or other children make every day.

Photocopiable activity sheet 1

This sheet is for lower ability children. It shows scenarios where a decision has been made. The children must decide whether the decision that was made was right or wrong. They should write down a reason for their answer.

Photocopiable activity sheet 2

This sheet is for more able children. They are to consider decisions that have been made for them that they agree with and decisions that have been made for them that they don't agree with. They should write down why they feel the decisions they have identified are not fair and what they would prefer to have done. They are then asked to write about decisions they agree with and why they were correct.

Plenary session

As a class share the children's ideas and discuss the decisions they have written about. Encourage them to consider why decisions that they believe to be unfair are made by parents, guardians, carers and teachers. Are these decisions made out of concern for the child's safety and development or are they really just unfair?

◆ Right or wrong? ◆

◆ Look at the pictures. Then complete the sentences.

The boy should/should not eat the

food because

The girl should/should not go to bed

because

The girl should/should not go to

school because

The boy should/should not have

pushed the girl because

PHOTOCOPIABLE PAGE   **Hopscotch** ◆ Me as a person

◆ Right or wrong? ◆

◆ There must have been times when you have thought 'That's not fair!'

◆ Write about decisions that have been made for you that you think were unfair.

- _____
- _____
- _____

◆ What would you have liked those decisions to be?

- _____
- _____
- _____

◆ Now think about decisions that have been made for you that you agree with. Say why.

- _____

This was right because _____

_____

- _____

This was right because _____

_____

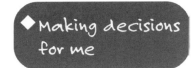

Making decisions for me

Intended outcomes

◆ The children will begin to realise that they have a choice, that they can say no and the consequences of not making the right decision. They will begin to appreciate the importance of making an informed decision.

Resources

◆ the photocopiable activity sheets on pages 35 and 36

Lesson plan for older children

Introduction

◆ Introduce the lesson by asking the children if they have ever had a friend who has done something that they have known to be wrong (some may raise their own experiences). If they do talk about someone else, stress that they should not mention names. Write some of these incidents on the board. The children might come up with issues of petty theft, bullying, telling lies, smoking and so on. Discuss with the children why they believe their friends made these decisions. What else could their friends have decided to do instead? Write up the alternatives on the board next to the decisions.

◆ Ask the class whether or not they feel their friend (or they) was pressured into making the decision or was it purely their own idea? Have the children heard of the term 'peer group pressure'? Explain to them what it means.

Group activities

Photocopiable activity sheet 1

This sheet is for lower ability children. It contains a decision tree which asks them to consider the consequences of making the right and the wrong decisions in given situations. The children will complete the tree showing the decisions they think they would have made. When they have completed their sheets, the children could compare their decisions with a friend and discuss the consequences.

Photocopiable activity sheet 2

This sheet is for higher ability children. They are asked to read the start of a story about a boy who goes off to play with some friends in a busy supermarket car park. His mum thinks he is going to play in a friend's garden. The children have to consider the story and write notes on Louis's behaviour, reactions and decisions. They then have to finish the story.

Plenary session

Share the children's decisions on the decision tree and discuss them. Read some of the story extracts from Activity sheet 2 to the whole class. Ask some of the children who completed Activity sheet 2 to say why they think Louis made the decisions he did. Discuss whether he made the right decisions. Consider the nature of peer group persuasion and the pressure to conform. Ask a couple of the children to read out their story endings. What decisions did they make for Louis?

(This lesson could be developed at a later stage with the children writing more of this story or a similar one.)

◆ Making decisions ◆

You have been asked to go
to the shops. Do you…

| Ride a bike? |

Why? _____
_____
_____

| Walk? |

Why? _____
_____
_____

| Do you decide to ride your bike in the middle of the road? |

| Yes | | No |

Why? _____
_____
_____

| You get to a crossing. Do you look carefully before you cross? |

| Yes | | No |

Why? _____
_____
_____

| You get to the shops. Do you decide to leave your bike unlocked? |

| Yes | | No |

Why? _____
_____
_____

| You get to the shops. Do you pat the dog that is tied to the post? |

| Yes | | No |

Why? _____
_____
_____

| You find £5 on the ground. Do you keep it? |

| Yes | | No |

Why? _____
_____
_____

| You find some sweets. Do you keep them? |

| Yes | | No |

Why? _____
_____
_____

◆ Making decisions ◆

◆ Read through this story and answer the questions.

Louis woke up one Saturday morning. He was excited. He was going to hang out in the carpark at the supermarket with his friends. His mum thought he was going to play with Martin in his back garden. She didn't like his other friends very much.

Why do you think Louis was excited?

Louis ate his breakfast and rushed out of the house, shouting to his mum that he was off to Martin's. As he got close to the supermarket, he started to feel a bit nervous.

Why do you think Louis was nervous?

Then he saw Hayley pushing an empty trolley around the carpark, shouting 'Get out of the way, Grandad!' at a man who was putting his shopping in his car. The man dropped his eggs and stepped towards her, frowning. But then he got in his car muttering 'Pesky kids'. Louis laughed with Hayley because he felt he should. But he was beginning to feel uneasy. 'Come on, Louis,' shouted Hayley. 'Let's go!' Louis felt sick.

Why did Louis think he should laugh with Hayley?
Why was he beginning to feel uneasy?

◆ What were the different decisions Louis made that day?

_____

_____

_____

◆ On the back of this sheet, write the end of the story. What decision did Louis make in the end?

◇ ◆ ◇ ◆ ◇ ◆ ◇ ◆ ◇ ◆ ◇ ◆ ◇ ◆ ◇ ◆ ◇ ◆ ◇ ◆ ◇ ◆ ◇ ◆ ◇ ◆ ◇ ◆

 Hopscotch ◆ Me as a person

Further activities to develop understanding

◆ Brainstorm the challenges we have to face as children/young adults/adults. Do the challenges change as we grow older? Brainstorm what the challenges for the children might be. These could be at home or at school. For example, they could include changing school, moving house, the loss of a member of the family or living with a new family.

◆ Ask the children to put together questionnaires relating to the personal, social and global issues discussed in the activity above. These could include questions asking: how the children feel about personal concerns, such as changing schools; about issues they are concerned with at a local level, such as litter; about issues that concern them at a national level, such as the increasing amount of traffic on the roads; and about issues that concern them at a global level, such as pollution. When the questionnaires have been completed, collate the findings on to one large sheet of paper and display it. This will represent the concerns of the class.

◆ Brainstorm what choices the children have to make or have made for them, every day at home or at school. What choices do their parents/carers/teachers have to make? What choices are made for them? How much control do we have over the choices we can make? Why is this? What action can the children take? See the generic sheet on page 61.

◆ Identify specific choices that have to be made and discuss the effects that media, peers, teachers and family members have on the outcome of those decisions. For example, what choices do we make that are influenced by what we see on television? Discuss the impact of advertisements for foods, drinks, clothes, toys and so on. Do any of the children buy products featured in the advertisements? Why? Do they think advertisements tell them the whole truth? Discuss decisions made about what to buy that are affected by our friends, family and teachers. These could be about why the children think playground trends, such as collecting and swapping famous character cards and stickers, are so successful.

◆ When we are faced with a decision we have to make, what strategies do we use to help us make our minds up? Complete a grid showing who decides issues. The children should identify the decision-makers in each situation. For example, who decides how much pocket money they receive? When the list has been completed, ask the children to select three decisions where the decision-maker is different each time. What constraints are the decision-makers under when they make that choice? Are they constrained by issues of safety, finance and legality?

◆ Investigate where the children can find information on issues that might have been raised, such as transfer to secondary school, moving house, bereavement, drugs, smoking, alcohol, relationships and puberty. Debate related issues, such as age limits.

◆Understanding a changing me

Focus

◆ Developing confidence and responsibility, and making the most of their abilities, pupils should be taught 1d) to recognise, as they approach puberty, how people's emotions change at that time and how to deal with their feelings towards themselves, their families and others in a positive way.

Key issue: What is happening to me and my friends? What is going to happen to me and my friends?

◆ Puberty is when children begin to change into adults.
◆ Puberty occurs at different times and at a different rate in all children.
◆ Children need to be educated about the changes that are going to happen to them.

Notes for teachers

When a child reaches puberty, their physical, mental and social states begin to develop into those of a young adult. These changes may begin at different times within the child and generally occur earlier in girls than boys. Today a surprising number of girls will have started puberty by the age of eight. This can make things very tricky for the teacher and these children should be handled with sensitivity.

When a child is earlier or later to reach puberty than his or her friends this can lead to frustration, embarrassment or even shame. Children often feel very self-conscious about their stage of development. They sense exclusion from the majority of their peer group by something that is out of their control.

At the same time as feeling and recognising that they are becoming different, those starting puberty may also begin to feel other emotions and experience mood swings that they might not be able to recognise or cope with. They may become upset and start to cry for no apparent reason or they may suddenly become angry and uncooperative. These new feelings only make the children feel more self-conscious, awkward and embarrassed.

Adults traditionally have thought of adolescents as surly and uncooperative teenagers and dismissed their problems as 'growing up'. As we become aware of the increasing number of very young children starting puberty, we will need to become more sympathetic.

All children need to be handled with sensitivity as they approach and go through puberty. We need to give them the skills, knowledge and understanding to deal not only with their own development, but to recognise that their peers are developing too, possibly at different rates to themselves. We must give them the confidence to understand that what is happening to them is normal and nothing to worry about.

We advise that if you are unsure about the teaching of this module, you check your school policy for Health and for PHE.

◇ ◆ ◇ ◆ ◇ ◆ ◇ ◆ ◇ ◆ ◇ ◆ ◇ ◆ ◇ ◆ ◇ ◆ ◇ ◆ ◇ ◆ ◇ ◆ ◇ ◆ ◇ ◆ ◇ ◆ ◇ ◆ ◇ ◆ ◇

Intended outcomes

◆ The children will develop their understanding about a range of emotions and will begin to recognise that as they get older the range of emotions they feel and the situations in which they feel them, become more complex.

Resources

◆ the photocopiable activity sheets on pages 40 and 41

Lesson plan for younger children

Introduction

◆ Sit down for a circle time activity. Discuss with the children what they understand about emotions. After a few minutes, confirm with them that emotions are about the way that people feel inside. Emotions are feelings like anger, happiness, sadness, loneliness, joy, love, frustration and irritation.

◆ With sensitivity, choose two or three of these emotions and discuss them further around the circle with children sharing experiences about when they have felt these emotions or times when they think they might feel these emotions. Then open the discussion further by asking the children about the emotions they might have felt as babies. Would they have been the same or different to those they feel now?

Group activities

Explain to the children that they are to complete sheets that ask them to consider their developing emotions. They should reflect on their own experiences as they have grown older and identify characteristics of behaviour in specific circumstances.

Photocopiable activity sheet 1

This sheet is for less able children. They are asked to match emotions to situations and offer an explanation for their choice.

Photocopiable activity sheet 2

This sheet is for more able children who are asked to consider a broad range of emotions. They should consider when babies feel happy, sad and angry. They then reconsider these emotions and others as they grow older. The aim is to encourage them to reflect on their increasing emotional maturity.

Plenary session

Regroup the class as for a circle time session and ask them to consider whether the situations in which they felt the most basic emotions of happiness, sadness and anger have changed as they have grown older. For example, a baby will show happiness when it is given a bottle of milk. Young children would be less happy – their needs have changed and so have their expectations. As they grow older, they are no longer happy with what used to satisfy their needs because their needs have changed. Can they think why this change has taken place? Guide them towards a recognition that they are maturing.

◆ Feelings ◆

◆ Look at the pictures below. By each one write what
the emotion is and why you think this is happening.

This baby is _____ _because_ _____

_____

_____

_____

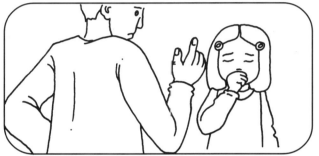

This girl is _____ _because_ _____

_____

_____

_____

This boy is _____ _because_ _____

_____

_____

_____

_____

This boy is _____ _because_ _____

_____

_____

_____

◆ On the back of this sheet, write what makes you happy, angry or sad.
Have you ever been shy? If so, when and what happened?

PHOTOCOPIABLE PAGE

◆ Feelings ◆

◆ Look at the pictures. Think about what causes our emotions. Complete the sentences. Draw yourself in the empty box.

A baby feels happy when _____
_____

A baby feels unhappy when _____

A baby feels angry when _____
_____

A small child feels happy when _____
_____

A small child feels sad when _____
_____

A small child feels angry when _____
_____

I feel happy when _____
_____

I feel unhappy when _____
_____

I feel angry when _____
_____

Adults feel happy when _____
_____

Adults feel sad when _____
_____

Adults feel angry when _____
_____

Intended outcomes

◆ The children will consider and reflect on emotions that they experience and will begin to recognise when other people experience the same emotions. The children will be encouraged to reflect on situations and to acknowledge that their actions affect the emotional experiences of others.

Resources

◆ the photocopiable activity sheets on pages 43 and 44

Lesson plan for older children

Introduction

◆ Seat the whole class as for a circle time activity. Lead a discussion about what emotions are, the emotions the children are aware of and the situations in which they feel them. For example, what makes them feel angry or frustrated and what do they do that makes other people feel angry and frustrated? The pictures on the photocopiable sheets could be blown up to A3 size and used as a focus point for the class throughout the lesson.

Group activities
Using the photocopiable activity sheets

Tell the class that they are going to work in pairs, studying and discussing four pictures. The children are to look at the pictures closely and try to work out what is going on in each. They should then write down details about what they think is happening around the outside of each picture. Ask them to think about the following questions:

◆ Who is in the picture?
◆ What happened just before the picture was drawn?
◆ What should happen next and is this different to what will happen next?
◆ How do the people in the picture feel about themselves and any others in the picture?

If they are struggling for ideas you might suggest the following:

Frightened – Can they see someone in danger? Is a parent/carer in difficulty? Are they frightened of something, such as a spider? Has a parent/carer driven off without them?

Sad – Is someone they love leaving them? Have they seen an accident? Are they homesick? Is someone they love poorly?

Happy – Are they going to a party? Is it the start of the school holidays? Are they happy to be returning to school? Is someone arriving who they have been looking forward to seeing?

Angry – Has someone bullied their friend? Has someone been unkind or cruel? Have they been blamed for something that was not their fault?

(You may prefer to have the whole class discussing the pictures rather than them going away to work on them.)

Plenary session

Discuss with the class whether they have ever found themselves in the situations shown in the pictures. Can they share with the class how they felt at the time and how the situation was resolved? Are there any who are prepared to admit that they caused a situation that has led to others becoming upset? Can they share with the class how they felt at the time? What was it that made them behave in such a way? If you have displayed enlarged versions of the pictures on the photocopiable sheets, you could invite children to come up and write their thoughts on the pictures.

◆ How are they feeling? ◆

◆ Look at the pictures. What is happening? Write your ideas around the pictures.

Why?

Why?

◆ How are they feeling? ◆

◆ Look at the pictures. What is happening? Write your ideas
around the pictures.

Why?

Why?

PHOTOCOPIABLE PAGE **Hopscotch** ◆ Me as a person

Further activities to develop understanding

◆ Arrange an anonymous suggestion box for questions that pupils might want to raise and have answered about puberty and the way they are feeling.

◆ Ask the children to consider who their friends are and what they like about them. They could think about how they can tell what their friends are feeling. How do their friends behave/look/ sound when they are happy/sad/angry and so on. See the generic sheet on page 64.

◆ Ask the children to write down five different moods they have been in and the situations they were in that brought these moods on. What did they do to bring themselves out of these moods?

◆ The children could consider what their parents expect of them as they grow older. They should be encouraged to recognise that as they mature, the expectations placed on them will become greater. See the generic sheet on page 63.

◆ Lead class discussions about issues such as vandalism, bullying, racism and sexism. Also consider an invitation to experiment with: drugs, smoking, relationships and sex. Can the children discuss how they would cope with people persistently asking them to do something they consider to be risky? Develop these situations through role play scenarios.

◆ When I was young I used to feel sad when... I used to feel happy when... I used to feel worried when... I used to feel angry when... Draw pictures and write to describe each emotion. As an extension the children could write about what makes them feel these emotions now.

◆ Ask the children to make dictionaries of words relating to their emotions. They should think carefully about the definitions.

◆ As a class, create a big book of stories and poems describing feelings. This could be put together over a period of time.

◆A money-minded me

Focus

◆ To develop self-esteem, confidence, independence and responsibility and make the most of their abilities, pupils should be taught to look after their money and realise that future wants and needs may be met through saving.

Key issue: The children should learn about how money works, its value, its uses and its associated responsibilities.

In doing so, they must appreciate:
◆ why money is necessary in our society
◆ where money comes from
◆ who makes decisions about how the money is spent
◆ how to get value for money
◆ how to ensure that the money we have is spent wisely
◆ the importance of saving as a way of securing our needs in the short and long term

Notes for teachers

Children must learn to appreciate the value of money from a young age. They must begin to appreciate that, when they have money, there are important choices to be made. Throughout Key Stage Two this could involve deciding to save to purchase a wanted possession as a short-term project. As they grow older, saving should be encouraged as a way of meeting individual and group wants and needs.

The wants and needs of a child change as they grow older. At a very young age, a child might be interested in buying sweets and small toys. As they grow older, they are going to be interested in buying clothing, fashion accessories, CDs and so on. As young adults looking after themselves, they will need to provide money for accommodation, food and drink, suitable clothing, transport, entertainment and other general expenses. We must teach our young children that if they choose to spend all their money at once on sweets, they will be unable to provide sufficient funds for larger items.

Children should be taught how they can save money. This can start with a discussion about piggy-banks, the first experience they may have had with saving their money. It would be useful to hold a discussion on the ways that children can save through banks, building societies and Post Office accounts. Children should be encouraged to realise why people save their money.

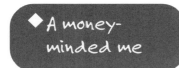

Intended outcomes

◆ The children will learn about the importance of not spending all their money in one go. They will learn that they have choices and that they have to live by the consequences of the choices they make.

Resources

◆ various coins and notes
◆ the photocopiable activity sheets on pages 48 and 49

Lesson plan for younger children

Introduction

◆ Hold up an amount of money and ask the children 'What is this?' Discuss with them the coins and notes they are aware of. Then ask them what they do with their money. Write their answers on the board.

◆ Hopefully, some of the children will say 'save it' and a discussion could follow on saving money. This discussion should look at the reasons why children save money and where they are able to save money. Do any of the class have piggy-banks, building society accounts, bank accounts or Post Office accounts? (If the children do not mention saving, trigger the discussion by asking what 'saving' means.)

◆ When the discussion has been completed, refocus the children on the brainstorm on the board. Now discuss how much money they think should be spent on the items listed on the board. Do they think the recommended amounts are sensible or unrealistic?

Group activities

Tell the children that they have two pounds to spend at the weekend. In pairs, they should discuss how this money could be spent wisely and unwisely. Explain that they are going to complete two shopping lists. One is for an unwise child who spends all her money on crisps and chocolate. The other is for a sensible child who buys a drink and some sweets, but also saves some money for another day.

Photocopiable activity sheet 1

This sheet is for less able children. They just have to list items that they think the two children would buy. A word bank is provided to help them complete the sheet.

Photocopiable activity sheet 2

More able children have two shopping lists to complete. They should explain why their choices were made.

Plenary session

Invite the children to share their lists with the class. Discuss why the lists were sensible or unwise. Go on to stimulate a discussion with the children on any purchases they have made that they regretted (such as 'trendy' or cheap toys that don't work or go out of fashion quickly). Discuss why it is important not to spend all your money at once.

◆ Mr Wise or Miss Unwise? ◆

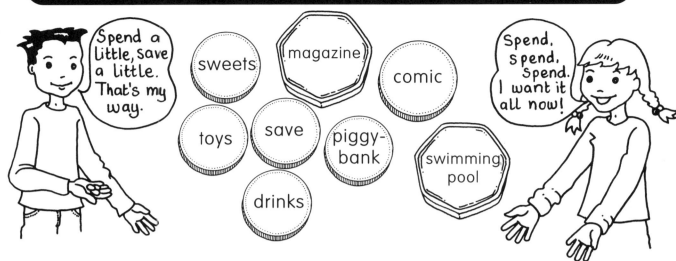

◆ Both these children have £2 to spend. What would a sensible person like Mr Wise do with his money? How would an irresponsible person like Miss Unwise handle her money? Write a shopping list for each of them. Remember – you cannot spend more than £2.

Mr Wise	Miss Unwise

◆ Mr Wise or Miss Unwise? ◆

◆ You have £3. Think about how you spend your money. Would you be like Mr Wise or Miss Unwise? Make out two shopping lists and explain why the money has been used in this way.

A wise person would _____

_____

_____

_____

_____

_____

An irresponsible person would _____

_____

_____

_____

_____

_____

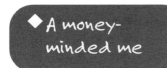

Intended outcomes

◆ Older children will reflect on the money they spend and on the importance of saving. They will begin to recognise that adults need money to provide for their everyday needs.

Resources

◆ the photocopiable activity sheets on pages 51 and 52

Lesson plan for older children

Introduction

◆ Introduce the lesson by telling the class what an adult spends their money/salary on, for example food, clothing, accommodation and living expenses, transport, entertainment – often for themselves and a family. Draw up a fictitious account on the board to illustrate the point.
◆ Ask the children to consider what they spend their money on during the day. They should discuss with a partner their financial day, starting, for example, with the bus ride to school.

Group activities

When they are reasonably confident they have remembered everything they should complete the first section on their photocopiable activity sheets.

Whole class

◆ After a few minutes bring the class back together and discuss some of the children's scenarios. Can they think of anything that has been missed out? Now ask them to complete the second part of their activity sheets.

Photocopiable activity sheet 1

This sheet is for less able children. The children have some simple questions to answer.

Photocopiable activity sheet 2

This sheet is for more able children who are asked to answer more complex questions.

Plenary session

Share the children's responses to the questions on the sheets. Discuss the importance of saving. Is there anything they think they would need to save for? To end the lesson, encourage them to consider whether the money they spend is the only money that will be spent on meeting their needs over the next seven days. What other money will be spent on them over the next seven days (food, clothing, accommodation and so on)?

◆ Money, money, money ◆

◆ How do you spend your money? Do you always spend wisely? Complete the chart below to show how much money you have spent in the last week. You can use a calculator.

Day	Items/amount	Total
Monday		
Tuesday		
Wednesday		
Thursday		
Friday		
Saturday		
Sunday		
Total for the week		

◆ Did you save any money? _____

◆ Look at how you spent your money. Do you think you spent it wisely? _____

◆ Why do you think this? _____

_____

◆ Why do you think people save money?

_____

_____

_____

◆ What would you like to save for? _____

◇ ◆ ◇ ◆ ◇ ◆ ◇ ◆ ◇ ◆ ◇ ◆ ◇ ◆ ◇ ◆ ◇ ◆ ◇ ◆ ◇ ◆ ◇ ◆ ◇ ◆ ◇ ◆ ◇ ◆ ◇ ◆ ◇

◆ Money, money, money ◆

◆ How do you spend your money? Do you always spend wisely? How much money have you spent in the last week? Complete the chart below.

Day	Items/amount	Total
Monday		
Tuesday		
Wednesday		
Thursday		
Friday		
Saturday		
Sunday		
	Total	

◆ Look at your chart. How much money did you spend wisely? Explain.

_____

Did you waste any money? _____ Did you save any? _____

◆ Write a short paragraph about why you think saving is or is not important.

_____

_____

_____

_____

◆ On the back of this sheet, write how you think we could encourage people to save more and to spend their money wisely.

Further activities to develop understanding

◆ Hold a general discussion with the children on what they spend their money on. Show them photographs from a contrasting country and discuss what the people in the photographs might spend their money on.

◆ Discuss with the children what can and can't be bought. For example, friendship cannot be bought, but sweets can be.

◆ Discuss with the children the saying 'Money is the root of all evil'.

◆ Ask the children what they would buy for themselves and how they would go about saving the money in order to be able to afford it.

◆ Discuss with the children the importance of securing employment in order to earn money.

◆ Discuss with the children the difference between what they need and what they want.

◆ Organise a pretend shop for a maths session. Working in pairs, one child is the shopper, the other works the till. They must calculate the price of the shopping and the amount of change to be given.

◆ The children could organise and run a stall raising money for a local or national charity or cause.

◆ Undertake an investigation into the value of money through history. What different currencies have been used? What was the value of £1 in Victorian times?

◆ Research and display the different currencies from around the world. Use the generic sheet on page 64.

◆ Confidence ◆

◆ Read the beginnings of the statements below. Write around each cloud your thoughts about the statements.

When I am confident I feel...

I feel confident when I...

I don't feel very confident when I...

My parents/carers could help me feel more confident by...

My friends could help me feel more confident by...

My teachers could help me feel more confident by...

◆ On the back of this sheet, write about a time in your life when you felt most confident. Draw a picture to illustrate it.

PHOTOCOPIABLE PAGE

◆ Different types of jobs ◆

◆ With a friend, talk about the different jobs you know about and write them around the tractor.

◆ Now decide whether these jobs are in the service, commercial, entertainment or manufacturing sectors. Write them around the boxes below .

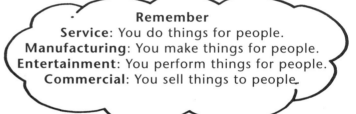

Remember
Service: You do things for people.
Manufacturing: You make things for people.
Entertainment: You perform things for people.
Commercial: You sell things to people.

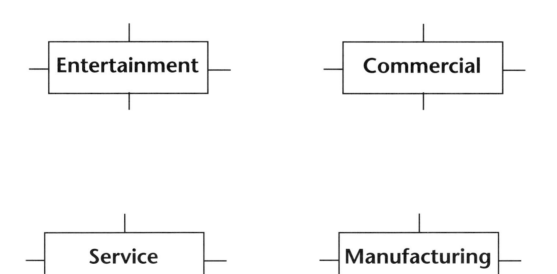

Entertainment

Commercial

Service

Manufacturing

◆ On the back of this sheet, write the job you want to do when you grow up and which sector it will be in. Draw a picture of yourself doing this job.

◆ Job application form ◆

Name: _____

Date of birth: _____

Address: _____

_____

Position applied for: _____

Relevant qualifications (please list most recent first):

_____   _____

_____   _____

Relevant experience:

_____

_____

_____

Why do you think you would be good at this job?

_____

_____

_____

What are your hobbies and what do you enjoy doing?

_____

_____

_____

◆ Points of view ◆

◆ Cut these cards out along the dotted lines. Turn the cards upside down and let the children pick the topics for discussion.

In order to grow fit, strong and healthy, all children should be made to walk to school.

In order to make sure they have a healthy and balanced diet, all children should eat school dinners.

In order that children learn how to talk and play with other people, they should spend less than one hour a day in front of the television and computer.

In order to encourage recycling, all families should use three bins: one for paper, one for glass and one for other household waste.

In order that children spend as much time at school as possible, families should not take holidays in term time.

Children should be allowed to do whatever they like because it is important to keep them happy.

◆ About me ◆

◆ Draw pictures and complete each of these sentences.

These are things you can feel pleased about.

| | I am good at: _____ _____ _____ _____ | | I enjoy doing: _____ _____ _____ _____ |

| | I take care of: _____ _____ _____ _____ | | I enjoy doing: _____ _____ _____ _____ |

Now think about these.

| | I want to get better at: _____ _____ _____ | | I don't enjoy: _____ _____ _____ _____ |

| | I need to take more care of: _____ _____ _____ | | I don't like talking about: _____ _____ _____ |

◆ Emma's dilemma ◆

Emma sat down to breakfast. She took a deep breath and picked up the spoon. How she hated cereals. Why did her mum insist that she eat them every day when she must have told her a hundred times that she would rather have toast? She forced the cereals down knowing that not to eat them would lead to 'words' with her mother.

She put her coat on and collected her bag from the table in the hall. She turned to look over her shoulder to make sure that she was not being watched. Then she tiptoed into the living room, took Harry, her hamster, from his cage, opened her bag and slipped him inside. She knew that Harry must miss her as much as she missed him when she was at school. She was sure that he would be quite safe in her bag – no-one need ever know he was there.

At school, she hung up her coat in the cloakroom and placed her bag on the peg. She felt inside her bag to make sure that Harry was safely tucked inside but just at that moment the shrieking of the school bell startled her and as she jumped slightly backwards her bag fell to the floor and Harry jumped out.

What was she going to do now? If she tried to find him she would be late and have to explain where she had been. If she told someone she had lost him she would get into trouble for bringing him into school. And if she left him she had no idea

◆ Emma's dilemma ◆

what might happen to him. Her friend Isaac beckoned to her to hurry up. As she went to the classroom she kept her eyes peeled to the floor. She had her fingers crossed hoping that she would find Harry before anyone else did. Unfortunately, she bumped straight into two children coming in the opposite direction. As she fell to the floor she stumbled into three other children who in turn knocked over a table that had on it a vase of flowers. The vase smashed to the floor spilling water everywhere.

Mr Singh was sitting at his desk marking books when he heard the huge noise. As he was about to step outside the classroom he saw a small furry creature run into the remains of a smashed vase that was on the floor. A small boy screamed 'Look! Look! A rrrraat!'

'Where, where?' yelled a group of children who had come along to see what was going on. Mr Singh, looking at the scene in front of him, decided to take charge. The children were now becoming hysterical at the thought of the gigantic rat that was freely roaming their school. Emma knew who the rat really was but if she owned up she would be in terrible trouble, especially now.

Mr Singh clapped his hands and asked for quiet. He stepped over a child lying on the floor and stooped down. He carefully picked up a terrified Harry out of the debris. 'Does this creature belong to anyone?' he asked. Emma decided that she had better own up before she caused any more problems. If only she had not decided to bring Harry to school.

PHOTOCOPIABLE PAGE

◆ Decisions ◆

◆ Think about all the decisions that are made for you every day. What decisions do you make for yourself? What decisions do your parents or teacher make? Record them below.

◆ A changing me ◆

◆ Think of three ways in which you have changed since you were born.

1. _____

2. _____

3. _____

◆ As you grow older you will change in many different ways. Complete the pathway to show what changes you think will take place. Write your age in the circles and write sentences in the boxes.

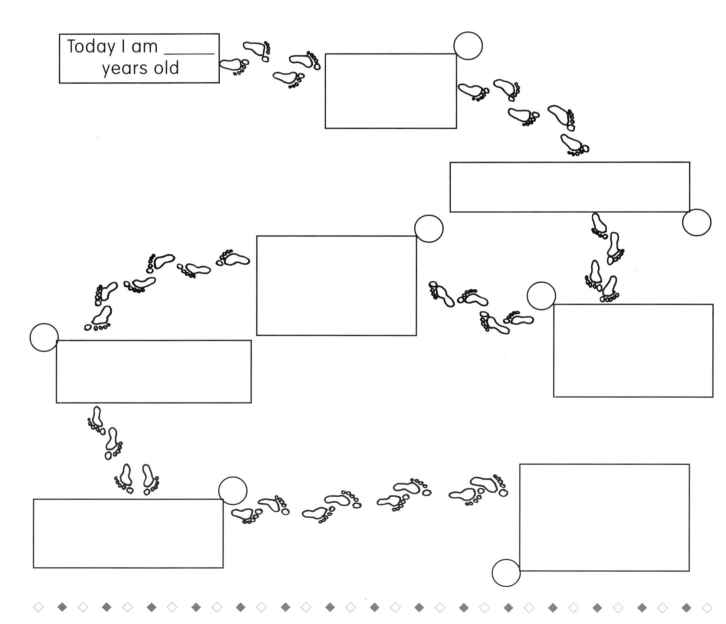

Today I am _____ years old

PHOTOCOPIABLE PAGE

Hopscotch ◆ Me as a person

◆ My friend and me ◆

This is a picture of my friend.

His/her name is _____

He/she is _____ years old.

I like _____ because

_____

_____

When _____ is happy he/she looks like this.

He/she behaves like this _____

_____

and sounds like this _____

_____

When _____ is unhappy he/she looks like this.

He/she behaves like this _____

_____

and sounds like this _____

_____

When _____ is angry he/she looks like this.

He/she behaves like this _____

_____

and sounds like this _____

_____

◆ On the back of this sheet, write down what **you** look like, behave like and sound like when you are happy, unhappy and angry. Talk about this with a friend.

◆ Money around the world ◆

◆ Find out the name of the currency in the countries listed below. You could use a newspaper, the Internet, an encyclopedia, visit a travel agent or ask a friend or relative.

France _____   Brazil _____

Germany _____   South Africa _____

America _____   Spain _____

Pakistan _____   Mexico _____

China _____   England _____

Denmark _____   India _____

◆ Choose six of these countries and use a newspaper or television to find out how much of their money you can get for £1.

1.   For £1 I can get _____

2.   For £1 I can get _____

3.   For £1 I can get _____

4.   For £1 I can get _____

5.   For £1 I can get _____

6.   For £1 I can get _____

◆ What other currencies do you know? Write about them on the back of this sheet.

PHOTOCOPIABLE PAGE   Hopscotch ◆ Me as a person